MUSINGS OF PERFECT MOONLIGHT

ANKITA SINGH

The book entitled " Musings of Perfect Moonlight is dedicated to Goddess Saraswati and my parents Mrs. Madhu Yadav and Mr. Hemant Kumar.

Contents

Acknowledgements

My heartiest thanks to my mother Mrs. Madhu Yadav , her adorable teachings of humanity in life inspired me to write poems on nature and other topics.

My heartiest thanks to my father Mr. Hemant Kumar his guidance in every step of life made me to think, reflect and understand each tiny phenomena, ups and downs of life and use them as a topics of poetry in arena of my writings.

My heartiest thanks to publisher, to publish my manuscript in book format.

Ankita Singh

Author Biography

Ankita Singh

Ankita Singh is indie author and freelance writer native to Lucknow , Uttar Pradesh, India. She is born poetess. After completing her graduation in Mass communication and video production she has earned degrees in Masters in journalism and Mass communication, B. Ed, M. Ed from university of Lucknow.

Her thirst for education further encouraged her to pursue M. A. English and M. A. Education from Dr. Ram Manohar Lohia Avadh University, Ayodhya, Uttar Pradesh.

She has qualified UGC NET in subject education 6 times.

She has also worked as an lecturer in a reputed university.

Till now her 12 books entitled " Kalam ke palash, chahakte panne, savan ke Hastakshar , Kavya ke Gulmohar " as a collection of her poems in Hindi , Poetic feathers as collection of poem in English.

"Shunya sarovar , Sneh Taru " books on short stories Hindi edition, " Tenses : The blossoms of English grammar " based on English curriculum, further sparrows Fiesta as a reference book English edition, "festive candles based on art and photography has been published. Two more books related to curriculum has been published.

Till now her 109 poems has been published in reputed books and magazines. She has also contributed her writings to research journals of National and International level.

Her area of interest includes educational psychology and research in education. A delight towards glittering lights makes her to play with wax and make decorative candles.

To touch the humanistic approach of her life, main aim of Author is to provide love, care and healthy environment to stray animals to let them survive with dignity on earth.

Email id – anks26.as@gmail.com

1. Dear Evening

Rain is dancing,
In charming monsoon.
You should come soon.
As a little delight to my heart.
For carrying pinkish blush,
In envelope full of happiness kart.

Envelope Image source: Internet

Just to steal fragrance of Rosemary flowers .

In tiny droplets of showers.
Rain is cooling ,
The burning noon.
You should become moon.
Just to steal blush of night with spark of stars.
Just to let me revive sound of unheard guitar.
Filling my empty feelings with musings ,
Of perfect moonlight.
As a charm of delight in veil of forgotten me.
Just to let me see some dreams again.
Just to regain fading me in myself.

Yours Ankita

2. Gulmohar tree

Hi , human
Receive my hail.
To hear the pleasing tale .
Of our lovely bounding .
In courtyard of your surrounding.
I was standing a decade long .
To sing a love song of love birds.
To let my branches become your swing.

Branches of treeImage source: Internet

To greet moon in valentine night.
To hold your love kite
stuck in my leaves.
beautiful name of your beloved was engraved in my trunk ,but
. . . .
Your heart suddenly shrunken.
You bought axes and sword.
To cut our love cords.
To cut my leaves , branches and trunk.
To destroy me till my end.
My destruction is mourning verse.
To give you a tiny curse.
You will suffer with destruction of tree.
May not receive oxygen for free .
In scorching heat of summer ,
You and your whole race will suffer.
From hot sun burn that leads to global warming.
Then you will remember my presence was too charming.
It was greeting verse to welcome rain.
To reduce Maina bird's pain .
She in search of rest ,
Made her nest .
In my arms .
To peak grain from your little palms.
But . . . .

You man forgotten humanity song ,
Just cut a Gulmohar tree
Which was a decade long .
A decade long......

Ankita Singh

3. Just a women

Far from us,
Sometimes me
Can see
Self esteem, courage and confidence.
As an evidence
Of my self realization.
To open the door of my inner voice,
With key of my choice.
A choice to touch sky.
A choice to fly high.
A choice to become blushing moon.
In dusty summer noon.
A choice to become stars
To remove all scars from worksheet of my destiny.
A choice to dive deep in ocean of myself
Where I can understand me well,
To not allow anyone to make my life hell.
Not just imperfect me,
As I'm she ,

SheImage source : Author

Who can write the verses
Of my name
As a fame in world.
Bcoz I'm women,
I ' m women.
As blossoms of fresh flower

To shower,
Love care and worth.
On earth
Just too need love, care and respect.
As my wages.
But Not the cages.

CageImage source : Internet

Of society.........
So think twice before uttering voice,
She is just a women.

Ankita Singh

4. Wings of literacy

Bangles in hand can hold pen.

PenImage source: Internet

Just to write her story,
On spark of success &
Revive freedom.
To celebrate ,
Independence in her .
As a golden fur,
Which owns prettiest skylark.
Singing in dark.

To mark,
Letter of great achievement in sky.
Let each girl fly high , fly high.
By owing self efficient wings of literacy.
Just to create her own legacy.

Ankita Singh

5. Winter Solstices

Ink of my love,

Turns pink.

To make your blue,

A story new.

Just like a new path of life.

For regaining lost me in yourself.

Asking for help,

To let me get drown.

At shore of your smile.

Just like a river Nile.

Tends to flood desserts of Egypt.

Same as your eyes flooded my heart.

Who are you?

Let me introduce.

You are winter solstice,

Came to make my dream realistic.

Forced me to fall in love with December snow.

Just to give January a vow,

To let February tie pink ribbon in my hair .

To let my blushing cheeks shy in cheer.

To mesmerize love foe winter solstices.

Ankita Singh

6. Fill in the blank of my life

Dreams of full moon.
Is charming boon,
To darkest night of new moon.
Just dancing in emptiness of unheard voice.
To rejoice,
The simple I and you.
In spirit of we,

Image source: Author we

Too see,
Spring of love in feelings of autumn.
To measure priceless fathom of your blush.
Just wrapped in pinkish red dimple of cheek.
To make me a freak,
Of your dazzling charm.
My dear prince charming.

Come and fill in the blank of my life.

Ankita Singh

7. Mother

In hot summer noon ,
She is winter solstice
To make my dreams realistic.
She is blush of full moon.
A wish of a divine boon.
She is no other than my mother,
Like a innocent feather of dove.
Flourished with treasure full of love .
Spreading the blessings with worthy hands.
She is like pure Ganges in dessert of sands .
A ray of hopeful light ,
In my all delight .
She is my wings
Each colourful flight.
I love , care and adore her,
She is my full life.

Ankita Singh

8. Musings of Rain

Musings of rain ,
Is happiness of heart.
To adore joy in natural kart.
The tiny droplets,
Just like anklets,
Sings nostalgic song-
Of little childhood which,
Awaited too long .
Just to secretly tear notebook paper.
For sailing paper ship,

Paper shipImage source: Author

Towards ocean of rain.
To just gain,
Mesmerizing charm of monsoon.
In burning summer noon.
Musings of rain ,
Is natural art.
Drawn with joyful brush,
On canvas of heart.
It is like a beloved holding hand.
In thirsty dessert full of sand.
Just to write pleasant song ,

To fill heart with tiny droplets of love verse for unknown.......
.....................??? Prince charming.

Ankita Singh

9. Black board

The darkest thing on earth .
I' am of no worth.
Inauspicious attitude in me .
No one like to see.
I'am the color black.
Which almost lack,
The qualities of good soul but …..
But….
I utter in silent voice.
I too can rejoice.
If you cut prefix-
In from word auspicious.
I become auspicious.
As used in place of learning.
Achieving promotion as black board.

Black boardImage source : Internet

Teachers write on my forehead.
To let students understand & lead.
The life of prosperity .
So, how can I be bad.
I too is soul of auspicious tranquility.

Ankita Singh

10. Nature's Healing

Last night when I was about to sail.
A big fish whispered in hail.
Hi! Human I'm whale.

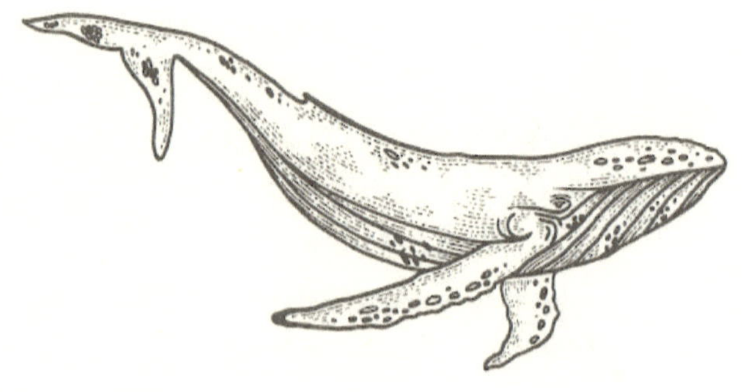

WhaleImage source: Internet

Just to share with you my shocking tale.
The fancy plastic bag you carry.
Makes my skin blue, black and pale.
It chocked my brother's lung.

A year back died the star fish and turtle.
Why you make our life hurdle.
By polluting river and sea.
Just come and see our drastic life .
We are struggling to survive.
Last night I saw with love .
A pair of dove.

spotted doveImage source: Author

Asking me for tiny grain.
Tiny eyes with full pain,
Seems to say,
Now where I should stay and rest.

As you men destroyed tree,
On which was my nest.
Why you human cut tree.
It provide you oxygen for free.
Last night I was talking to moon.
You are cool but why not noon.
It said, you human-
Self cursed your life.
Harshly disturbed climate &
eco- friendly life.
Now the earth is locked to global warming.
How can your life be pleasant and charming?
You will repent your greedy feelings.
Until you not support for –
Nature's healing , Nature's healing.

Ankita Singh

11. Golden name of Women

A women is pearl,
In ocean of life.
She is loving daughter ,

Women sketch Image source: Author

Sister and wife.
Full of love,
Like an innocent dove.
Just to sing song of care.
In each verse of her prayer.
She owns nothing of her own.

Her feelings are always unknown.
She needs a mirror of self-esteem.
To self realize her dreams.
To know she can touch sky&
Fly high .
Just like sky lark in darkest —
Night of winter solstices.
Just to make her achievements realistic.
To gain fame , embedded in golden name.
Golden name.

Ankita Singh

12. Sparrows

To serve humanity .
Is sole purpose of life .
Which men forget in strife.
To maintain harmonious relationship with nature.
To love care & respect every creature.
To allow little sparrows,

SparrowImage source : Internet

Accompany human surroundings.
To tie with them knot of cordial bounding.

To allow them to make nest ,
Where they can rest.
In ventilators near roof,
To show symbol of proof.
As human love sparrows.
They will live no long in danger.
They will never be endangered.

Ankita Singh

13. Where they should rest ?

Last night,
After mesmerizing the nostalgic childhood.
I again travelled to wood,

Quote on forest Image source : Nawab Wajid Ali shah zoological
Garden ,Lucknow

Near, my grand mothers home.
Where I can freely pick peacock feather,
In lovely monsoon weather.
Adoring tiny droplets of rain.
To just rub my pain .
In arms of my grandmother.
Keenly listening to story
Of my prince charming,
Hiding blush of my cheeks, which was heart warming.
I eagerly miss stories of thousand Mahua tree.
Once was de-rooted to make land free.

Quote on TreesImage source: Nawab Wajid Ali Shah zoological
Garden Lucknow, Uttar Pradesh

Just for construction of humanistic cities.
As a foundation of modernity.
Snatched forest pride,
which was adobe to wildlife.
A place where many animals can play and rest.
Tiny birds make nest.
Love bird tend to sing in spring.
To appraise elephant's wedding ring.
The uncle lion used to whitewash his den, but-
Greed of man cut their forest.
Now where they should rest?
Now where they should rest ?

Ankita Singh

14. Life is story

Life is a story
Of Ups and downs.
Just to fall deep & regain crown.
To build sea shore,
On chest of dessert.
To loose some treasure,
To gain big asset.
Just like an old cassette singing,

old cassette  *Image source : Internet*

Mute verse of struggle,
Motivating to achieve ,
Something great which may magnificently upgrade.
Value of human life,
On its highest drive.

Ankita Singh